Crone

Clare L. Martin

Nixes Mate Books
Allston, Massachusetts

Copyright © 2018 Clare L. Martin

Book design by d'Entremont
Cover photograph from the collection of Lauren Leja

All rights reserved. This book or any portion thereof may not be reproduced or used in any manner whatsoever without the express written permission of the publisher except for the use of brief quotations in a book review or scholarly journal.

Earlier versions of certain poems have appeared in *Nixes Mate Review* and *Unlikely Stories*. The author wishes to thank the lineage of living and dead poets who have inspired and encouraged her.

ISBN 978-1-949279-06-1

Nixes Mate Books
POBox 1179
Allston, MA 02134
nixesmate.pub/books

*And with a fist
I break earth to bury
in good mud, elemental
mothermud, dreams
their stomachs cannot hold.*

Crone

Blessing

lavender in a bowl
a berry on the tongue
the kiss of a queen
shepherds dreaming of seas
bells at the hour of prayer

perfume evaporating
and still, a residue of oil
on the inside of your wrist
ambergris and jasmine
a fig on the tree
chills in middle-night

rose petals and blood
in the palm of your hand
rain-heavy wings –
the last
muscle to grasp
      from a ragged heart

Here in the market,
children reap bones
of decayed mistresses.
A tongue, black as earth,
limps in the boy's mouth.
Beggars in thin robes
brim with insatiate hunger
for a stone to suck.
The hunchback carries sacks
        of blessed lime.

I was a ghostly infant;
breathless for milk –
A flaccid girl with no dowry.

My mother kindles joy
for the valuation in gold
she has been promised for me.
No life of foolishness.
No mother to inculcate grief.
My name – her tongue's amnesia.

Crone appears with a shield of lightning
and rose-scented balm for this captive wrist.
Her red right hand incised
        with a luminous eye.
I am now her possession.

Crone prepares the blackbirds
she gathered in nets.

Three carcasses on a plate.

All is gone, and I weep for nothing –
The nothing that is
and the nothing that was.

Too much to fear of a vagabond's life,
I do not know if I will survive.

        Rain brings the river to my mouth.

She told me to burn white candles to kindle inspiration
She told me to burn white candles to dissipate grief
She told me to burn white candles near a bowl of water
She told me to burn white candles to welcome ancestral
    spirits
She told me to burn white candles so I could be free
She told me to burn white candles at the birth of a child
She told me to burn white candles until the swallows
    return
She told me to burn white candles while lying with a lover
She told me to burn white candles *for the wine is bitter*
She told me to burn white candles to not forget
    the miscarried prayers
She told me to burn white candles – blazing wicks:
    an ablution of air
She told me to burn white candles to chart a nebula
    of horses
She told me to burn white candles as I hammer pain
    and anger
She told me to burn white candles to unmoor
    the salient heart

She is scantily-loved,
a rejected being of obtuse sex.
Clutching the solitary wish of freedom
redolent as an unleavened body.
Only through subjugation
will the reckoning culminate.

My winnowing begins.

My body on the wolf hide.
She lifts my skirt and collects
menses with a pewter spoon.
She transfers the clot into a chalice,
and adds the dust of chameleon skins,
fresh sage, and wild berry wine.

Drink only a mouthful. And now,
      we pour
the remainder on that earth
where you were brought into this world.

    This, the undoing.

a cronesong
of bitter-birthed children
unsleeping in palpable secrecy
anguish for a reunion of wounds
inhalation to exhalation
to salvation, the secret divulged
oh, humble solace of steadfast earth
reveal to us an exodus
to the craw of the volcano

Soul transmutes to obsidian –
       only then, absolution

As bitter silt washes
over your tongue,
*   name each child –*

Make an oblation
*   deep in the loam*
*   of your heart.*

Bury it so
even you will forget. Stare
into the void
*   of your cup.*

Do you see
their myriad deaths
*   in this cloak of dusk?*

She curls smoke with a knotted finger
and three times draws a clockwise
trail on the crown of my head.
She salts my tongue. I breathe in minute sips.
This will blind you, so you will see.
Fury erupts in the middlemost mind. A boy,
light-haired, shines in a sky black as the mountain.
A vulture plummets; annihilates him.
I begin to speak it –
      She silences me.

Wood-bare, waterless breasts, and a thistle's tongue
soul-huntress wolfbreath
a cascade of river legs
her lungs canter
with each inhalation
hoary-eyes bequeathed
by an uprising of toxic stone
magic, neither white or black,
wielded by wizened hand,
signifying the unpraised wealth
      of prophecy.

Silent in the grove,
she nails the hare to the tree.
Cuts a thin line and strips it.
Collects the innards
in an earthen bowl.
She splashes the headless
carcass with acrid vinegar.
Blade into the hind.
The swift knife cuts
by its own volition.
She washes the meat again.
Threads pieces on a spit.

As the fire grows,
she interrogates entrails
which portend
        a maelstrom of pregnancy.

Oh, tender one,
unravel your heart
Slip fingers
into the radiance
I have prepared for you
This kiss is the bitterest sea
This milk is the permutation
of a mother's malady
Sip it from earthen bowls
in a lush tent full of smoke
Once in my arms,
you will no longer fear
the retching years
There will be no more nights
lying with the bones
of desiccated lambs –
Cast off the tearless
children dying of thirst
Pick up your knife to sever
the moon from the sky!
She, whose vulva gesticulates
feverishly, is calling you
In my palm,
the heart collapses
from the weight

*of lived pain
No longer entwined
in the body
I will set you free
forever and ever and ever
from the incalculable
price of blood.*

The undulating core
of the universe encapsulated
in a most tender bulb of skin.
Her breath's ignition
resurrects the miracle nerve.

It is nothing like love,
it is nothing –
Be brave, she says.
It will hurt more than a little
 when I grind out the scars.

She shovels wet earth
with her bare heels.
Twists a windstorm
in her blossoming skirt.
Crone levitates to treetops,
cradles the moon in bewitched arms.
She descends to stones encircling fire.

    Ember and ash rain upwards.

She shows me his seed in a copper cup.

What do you see? She says.

I see white peaks
and the heraldry of white
horses, racing the sea.

> *Yes, yes.* She says. *Bring me his wife,
> and too, his mistress.*

Night is a bullion sea
edged in obsidian
into which we plunge.
A horizon obstructed
with seashell skeletons.
Incorporeal slights, the holy unbodied,
scrawl the weighted sun.
Sun's expiration is an incessant hiss.
My heart drains, refills –
      I cannot stop it!

Lark bones in the hedge.
The oaks form four corners.
She sprinkles dried feverfew
and mandrake to the north,
south, east, and west.
She pulls a silver strand
from the one braid of her long hair,
and sings the crow's caw.
She tucks the lark wings in her bosom.
Snaps the neckbone to preserve the skull.

Medicine for the maiden. A renaissance.

The old huntswoman
succumbs to a barrage of flies.
She unweaves the silver braid
and calls forth ancestral spirits.

She enters cavernous dreams.
Smoke blooms a cerulean haze.
Wood, hysterical, burns.
She breaks the vessel of a hawk's egg.
       Fires Palo Santo.

Dried blood flakes from her fingers.
A black tooth drops
       into the cauldron.

She asks me to salt her body
with that elemental blessing
we harvested from the brine
of the sea and purified with fire.

I coat my hands
with salt and chrism oil
then brush my palms on her skin.
From the crown of her head,
in the direction of blood flow
to the heart, which seems
to leap under my touch.

I stop at her heart for a moment,
and ask for release
of what her spirit has carried.

Her unskinned cry:
   helplessness, fear,
       ecstasy.

Those who will not stand must flee.
Gather what is useful, quickly –
Flesh to flower, all that is free.
Pray to half-light, pray to dark.
Leave at night, after rituals.
Go with the blessing
of the harrowed,
       mourned god.

evil
rends its tongue
with gritted cries
blood on the bough
a tarot tier
ineffable with dream
whispers
across moss
on my knees
to harvest a heart
in white woods
one shot
one arrow
pierces the doe
that fed on apples by the gate
rain and detritus of winter
a coyote alone
claws the mud
a stag sharpens venerable antlers
on the cleaved breast
of a five-hundred-year oak
hoofprints in snow
and silver grass
black, wet bark
blue-wet boulders

heathen succubae
haunt the grove
vulnerabilities of earth
and burning rivers
day-lit moon is a scar
hawks, the sky
snow buries
the chalice and the chain
royal blood
desiccated
strawberry crowns for the birds
death-keeper of desire
her keen sense perturbs
the physical world
grime haloes
albumen tongues
soft hoofbeats
white horses flee
a merciless fog
oak, cedar, cypress
vultures spiral
slag of gray clouds
candlewax sun
gold spears
the crone's sallow eye

A cockroach pulses
in her mouth
tomorrow's nowhere-grave:

a door
resolves all
that is pestilent

The corruption tremors
in the maiden's belly
like ringing metal.
The breathing ocean
bursts from the crag
of her womb. The wail of war –
she is marked and cannot go home.
Her mother fists the wall;
hunger-cries in the vortices of fetid air.

Be silent. Crone says. *It's gone.*

The fetus heart stops
in a globe of light
bones work
their way through flesh
flesh-in-water
her cheek depresses
a midwife's thumbprint
bruises aorta
gray washes into amber
soft, blooded veins –
her mother bears
the crown of thorns.

Desiccation we know
is truth
because the crone
layers each dream
upon the other
the crone dreams
these dreams for us
to show us
what happens

when men rise
when men fall.

When mothers suffer
up to their necks
reach for the ceiling
pray for lightning
      through the thatched roof:
a deliverance of a different kind
the ever-ghost children
quickly go to ground –

Beloved, loved,
      still-hearted and all.

*The dream comes from the sockets
and the eye itself,
(seer of all).
It comes from the marrow
and curses bone
into a galaxy of splinters.
It will reap the heart
and take the very last word
as it resounds upon utterance:*
                dust, dust, dust.

She combs my hair with the hollow
tip of a black vulture's feather.
and soothes my burning skin with fragrant oil.
She wraps me in silk, encloses me in her arms.
She whispers a prayer at my breasts
so that my heart can hear
        her profession of love.

I did not expect this kindness.

*One must turn themselves inside out
so that your heart drags from a rib.
You must eat your own shadow and drink dew
from the black mushroom that grows
out of the carcass of a dead stag.
Brew bitters distilled from rose thorn,
lichen – the matted duff of the forest,
        and a bit of gold.*

Unshackle your chastity.

*Three days in the lightless cave. No fire.
Consume an unleashed river.
Extinguish your dreams,
until the prophecy burrows
into your awareness, like a beetle or worm.
Speak a spell.
      (It is of no concern to you.)
Announce a deathly truth to the creeping fog.
Ascend the broken face of the mountain.*

Then you will be a wise woman.

Sand and salt mystify her visage.
The desolation of her eye – a heart-quake.

She has forgotten the feel of you.
Skin, muscle, bone, sex.

Curve and sunken-heart; shipwreck desire.
She prays at altars for the body's need.

Sacrifice upon sacrifice. Here
at the sea-edge, we've set fire to driftwood.

Temptress smoke, the holy kind –
We swirl in eddies of incantation.

The melancholic sea bulges.
Forgotten bone, flotsam, starfish –

starlight alien to Earth.
Lavish a blanket to shield the chill.

Skin-to-skin, we,
      now wordless,
           commune.

*Mercy, god of destruction –
All we are and ever will be
is want.*

A precise wind collapses.
Air fills with fluttering nymphs.
Angelic notes thrum in descending light.
    All traverses to black.
Only the immeasurable stars and *her eye*
    peer into sleep.

I go into the loam to sense what grows.
Stake myself to vine to flourish, root,
then rise unfurled, green and tender –
A lush frenzy. Swaths of mud at my mouth;
tongue-bloodied all for want
of aliveness, for seed, for newness,
birth and rebirth. And if it rains,
look for me dressed
in bright gowns of heaven.
Heart-drenched –
      full, open.

In the bitterest sea, she casts spells to draw a lover.
In the bitterest sea, she relinquishes stolen pearls.
In the bitterest sea, we discover a new life form.
In the bitterest sea, she recalls the child's death.
In the bitterest sea, verdant embryos bloom.
In the bitterest sea, voices drop to darkness.
In the bitterest sea, the wave wears a queen's jewels.
In the bitterest sea, hopes are ravaged.
In the bitterest sea, she drinks to fulfillment.
In the bitterest sea, we hunt glass bones.
In the bitterest sea, letters from the drowned surface.
In the bitterest sea, we swim in the moon's gasp.
In the bitterest sea, she tends the wound of night.

God's secret name must not be spoken.
And yet, you call upon it over and over,
when you're desperate to believe
you are free.

Dying, she is black lace and cedar,
the scum of rancid air, scarlet-flow on the plain.
Her smile is blowflies; her brow is utterly wracked.

I am forever her disciple.

Her malignancy imbues
a violence of scents:

> a blacksmith's burning,
> blood of the kill, ambergris
> and an extinguished lamp.

> She saws a path
wall-to-wall to whip-hard
bonebreak of hook, eyelid, nail –
I surrender the fear
that even now keeps me unbound to her.

Her salt in my nostrils,
salt on my tongue –

We lie between the five mounds
beneath the flowering pear.
Still, the wind gossips
> of summer grass.

Crone releases her last veil.
Her voice so soft I crane to her lips.
She uncoils a narrative of the lineage
of earth-binding women.
(Cries of babes, awakenings,
the guillotine and drownings,
a long poem so often dark).

Wet hair, white slip,
        sweat from the dance –

I draw ash over her head as blessing.

Crone says,

Glass bones cannot bear a body.
Tell no one
>*I am frail beyond the fragility of life.*

She is a phenom beam, translucent lungs, ice –

The whimpering prayer
empties from my breath.

The clock of the sky strikes six.
The Black Horse crosses the Indigo Bridge.
From thunderhead to branch,
her gaze drops to fevered fields.

    Night devours her sweet burning.

Sated with memory,
I cannot bear the lingering note
of her last breaths that haunt this stillness.
There was rage, too, in her mind's exodus.

I am left with the shackles.
They are so rusted
    I can almost break free.

Glowering god in the sacristy
enters wine, enters bread.
I fret against the pew.
Loaves of mourning and mirroring fish.
Women pass a collection plate.
Mercy, nailed feet and hands.
I kneel my prayer.
My bones ring redundancies
of sorrow –

Rend your garment
and ascend the cross.
Crucified, we become.

I cannot lift my eyes to this god
       and yet,
          in her perpetual eye,

I am clean.

I've been circling for thousands of years*
My skirts skim mountaintops.
Trees scrape my legs bone-branch raw.
At times, clouds part. Sometimes, they do not.
I favor thunderstorms –
the eerie kindness of hurricanes,
wrought with calm centers, the wind, and electric forces.
I've been circling for thousands of years,
planting seeds of conception.
I've been waiting for God to show a mighty hand.
I am an Old Woman, pregnant with ephemeral dust.

This is proof enough for me.

*a line by Rainier Maria Rilke

About the Author

Clare L. Martin's *Seek the Holy Dark* was selected as the 2017 Louisiana Series of Cajun and Creole Poetry by Yellow Flag Press. Her debut, *Eating the Heart First*, was published in 2012 by Press 53. Martin founded and edits the poetry magazine, *MockingHeart Review*. She lives in Louisiana with her husband and daughter.

42° 19' 47.9" N   70° 56' 43.9" W

Nixes Mate is a navigational hazard in Boston Harbor used during the colonial period to gibbet and hang pirates and mutineers.

Nixes Mate Books features small-batch artisanal literature, created by writers who use all 26 letters of the alphabet and then some, honing their craft the time-honored way: one line at a time.

nixesmate.pub/books

www.ingramcontent.com/pod-product-compliance
Lightning Source LLC
Chambersburg PA
CBHW052106110526
44591CB00013B/2369